Fly Cheap, Stay Cheap, Travel Cheap

By Ron Stern

Also by Ron Stern:

How to be a Travel Writer—the Easy Way!
Airfare GiveAway—How to Fly for Little or Nothing

Fly Cheap, Stay Cheap, Travel Cheap
Copyright 2010 by Ron Stern
Revised for 2015

Cover Design: S. Gefter
Photos: Ron Stern

Published Jan 2015

A Three Stars Press Book
New York   Fort Collins, CO   Los Angeles

Ron Stern is editor in chief of JustSayGo.com (www.JustSayGo.com), an online, travel-oriented e-zine. He is also the travel columnist for the San Diego Community Newspaper Group, Communities Digital News and 50 Plus Marketplace News. His articles have appeared in national and regional magazines such as *Shape, Cruise, Frequent Flyer, AAA Motorist, Visit Los Cabos Guide, Destinations West, Key Biscayne and La Jolla Today.* His other articles have been published in newspapers (print and online) such as *The Chicago Tribune, Orlando Sun Sentinel, Bismarck Tribune, The Jamaican Observer, the Coloradoan* and travel trade magazines. Ron's contributions have been noted by PBS, Mobil Travel Guides and his photography has been used extensively by entities such as tourism boards and public relations firms.

Visit his websites:

www.globalgumshoe.com
www.ronsternimages.com
www.facebook.com/globalgumshoe
www.youtube.com/globalgumshoe

Disclaimer

The information contained in this book is believed to be accurate as of the date of publication. Information (especially on the "information superhighway"), however, changes frequently so there may be errors and omissions. Make sure that you verify any information obtained from these pages with the actual provider, your travel agent, or from other sources. The author assumes no liability for damages suffered whole or in part from the information provided here.

Additionally, the discounts mentioned were obtained from Internet sources and in some cases by telephone with representatives from the service provider. Discount rates change as well, so you should also verify this information to make sure you're receiving current prices and discount structures.

Fly Cheap,
Stay Cheap,
Travel Cheap

Table of Contents

Preface

Like many people, my wife and I have always loved to travel. Unfortunately, two things usually stood in our way—time and money. When we had one, we frequently didn't have the other. Sometimes, on the rare occasions when the planets were aligned just right and we actually had both time and money together, we'd make a mad dash to the travel agent and book a trip. As we found out though—more than once—just because you use a travel "professional" doesn't always mean that things will go according to plan. Case in point. I planned a trip with some friends to a Mexican beach resort. We arrived late at night, tired from a long day's flight. I showed our reservations to the gentleman at the front desk of our hotel. He looked at it and, in broken English, said, "I don't have a room for you." We all looked at each other in disbelief. I tried again to show the clerk that we had a confirmed reservation through a travel agent. He just shrugged his shoulders and said he didn't have a room. The butterflies in my stomach were taking flight and I was asking myself, "And just why didn't I get the travel agent's home telephone number?" Since I hadn't had the foresight to do that, I turned to Plan B—our wives. (OK, maybe it was a chauvinistic response, but we were desperate!) Several minutes of sweet talk and fluttering eyelids, and, lo and behold, we suddenly found ourselves in "Room 18."

I later found out from others who had stayed at this same hotel that our reception was not at all unusual. "Oh yeah, we got room 18," declared one jolly regular. "They always try this with new people, hoping you will offer more money." Room 18 was painted a bilious shade of avocado green, was missing slats in the bathroom windows, and came equipped with a shower that just cried out for Ajax and bleach.

Despite the inauspicious start to the vacation, this turned out to be one of the best trips we'd ever had. I learned then—and since—that it is what you learn along the way that makes travel fun and exciting. Visiting new and unusual places—and even staying in a "Room 18"—makes for some great memories.

Years ago, you didn't have much choice when it came to planning your trip. You went to a travel agent, or you called an airline or a hotel directly. The Internet has changed all that. Now, with a few strokes of the keys, you can find the best water parks, the most unique museums, the most exotic cruises...whatever you want...and all at bargain (or at least discounted) prices. You can learn about local customs, flavors, and attractions before you leave. You can book on-line, e- mail questions on-line, and even take a virtual tour of your destination. And you can do all this from the comfort of your own home.

The trick is, knowing how to use the Internet for your advantage. In this book we have tried to compile the best sites, to give you the tools you need for creative travel. If you're ready, sit back at your computer, log on, and let the adventures begin.

Chapter One
Getting Started

Getting Started

For some of us, our travels really begin when we start the planning process. Choosing a destination, deciding how to get there and what to do once you do get there are all part of the fun. In the last few years, planning a trip has become that much easier with the help of the Internet. It can also be overwhelming too, especially if you're not used to navigating your way through cyberspace. I've chosen a few tried and true sites that we return to again and again...we think they'll help you too.

Fodor's www.fodors.com

Fodor's, a long-time travel planning mainstay, provides some of the best travel reviews and other information on the Internet. They offer special tips that, as of this writing included, how to stay healthy on the road, solo travel tips for women, five ways to save time at security, and how to travel with your pet. You can search for your perfect trip, find the latest news and features or search their seasonal travel picks.

Fly Cheap, Stay Cheap, Travel Cheap

Just Say Go www.justsaygo.com

This site has stories about many different travel destinations, both foreign and domestic. What makes this site fun and interesting is that it is written by travel writers and reads as if your best friend was describing her last great trip for you. There are also sections for photojournalism and festivals and events held throughout the world.

CNN Travel www.CNN.com/travel

CNN offers news about travel, the travel industry, as well as destinations, advisories, and top travel stories from around the world.

Concierge.com www.concierge.com

A spin off of Condé Nast Traveler, this website is designed for the sophisticated traveler. There are lots of nooks and crannies for you to explore. Their "interests" section for instance lets you browse by categories such as food and wine, family travel, cruises, beaches and islands, and more. They also have a nice destination and video section.

Trip Advisor www.tripadvisor.com

Trip Advisor offers unbiased advice on hotels, resorts and vacations. You can sign up to be notified of specials and this site will even help you plan your trip to almost anywhere. I especially like the link to reviews for various cities and destinations. Another way to use this is to simply use a search engine like Google and type in the name of any resort or hotel along with the words Trip Advisor. This should quickly bring up reviews by past travelers and will provide you with traveler's perspectives of the property. Anyone can post reviews on TripAdvisor so you too can become part of the travel community. They use a series of badges so the more reviews you write, the more you move up in ranking. It only takes 50 to become a top contributor.

Rough Guide www.roughguides.com

Rough Guides have become a standard item for many travelers and they currently have information on over 200 locations worldwide. They also have history guides, maps, restaurant guides, and phrasebooks for 18 languages. Check out their website for all the 'rough' information.

Rick Steve's Europe www.ricksteves.com

If you have seen any of his series on PBS then you know why. Rick travels all over the world and gives you his best tips for how to travel in Europe "through the back door." He leads guided tours,

Fly Cheap, Stay Cheap, Travel Cheap

publishes informative guidebooks, and even sells the type of "rucksack" that he recommends for his trips. My only question is: How can I get his job? Wait...I already have it!

Budget Travel Online www.budgettravel.com

This is an online version of Arthur Frommer's Budget Travel Magazine. It is loaded with useful information and penny-pinching specials. Archived articles cover everything from how to find the best deals on cruises to downloadable city guides. Sometimes what you can find on sites like this are package deals (airfare, hotels, taxes, fees) for the same price or lower than just the airfare alone to a destination. Recently, I saw a 7 night Ireland package from the east coast which included roundtrip airfare, 4 and 5 star hotels and a rental car starting at $699.

Lonely Planet Online www.lonelyplanet.com

Lonely Planet guides have been helping people find their ideal destination for many years. They have world guides, articles, and other helpful resources. If you have ever thought about trekking to some remote spot, chances are Lonely Planet has written about it.

Fly Cheap, Stay Cheap, Travel Cheap

The Travel Channel www.travelchannel.com

The Travel Channel website is a fantastic resource for all your travel needs. There are links and stories to practically everything you can imagine. Here are some examples:
*Royal Palaces to visit
*Where to stay on a Roman holiday
*Win a Lux vacation in Colorado
*Ways to vacation like a millionaire.
Of course they have a full lineup of Travel Channel shows. These are just a few of the hundreds of stories that can help you decide how to spend your summer vacation.

Travisa www.travisa.com

Need a passport fast? Then log onto Travisa. They can provide new passports, passport renewals, second passports, and even help with lost passports, sometimes in as little as 24 hours. They also can help with visa requirements and help you obtain one. You can also find rush passports at www.rushmypassport.com.

Currency Exchange
www.oanda.com/convert/classic

Okay, let's say you're going to Algeria and you have no idea what type of currency they use or the exchange rate. No problem. With just a couple of keystrokes, you can quickly find out how far your money will go in this part of the world. You can also purchase travelers checks on-line to be delivered right to your door. Another good site for this is www.xe.com/ucc/

Andrews Federal Credit Union
www.andrewsfcu.org

When I teach classes, the question always comes up as to the best ways to obtain money while traveling. Some people take all cash; others use ATM's or a combination of the two. The things that have to be considered would be safety in carrying cash, ATM fees including surcharges, foreign transactions fees, and more. Andrews Federal Credit Union has a no fee ATM card valid worldwide. What's more they offer a credit card called Global Trek Rewards that uses the more modern chip and pin technology which is common now throughout Europe. This card may come in quite handy, especially if you are trying to buy train tickets via an unmanned kiosk. The application process is a little time consuming but worth it for the benefits of these two products. Start by going online to their website to open a credit union membership and you can join one of their affiliate groups to get you into their system.

One Bag www.onebag.com

If you ever wondered how some people can pack everything they need in a single carry-on while you are towing several large crates of clothes, then look no further. This website is a treasure trove of information about everything related to packing including how to do it, what to take and product reviews of the best merchandise and deals.

CIA Fact Book
https://www.cia.gov/library/publications/the-world-factbook/index.html

The CIA—yes, that CIA—publishes a useful travel tool called their World Fact Book. You can find information about any country in the world related to topics such as economics, government, stability, and safety, to name a few. There are also handy, informative appendices and reference maps.

Air Ambulance Card
www.airambulancecard.com

Medical emergencies can happen at any time and in any place. Most insurance companies have a medical "necessity" clause that leaves the decision as to whether you need an airplane to fly you back to the U.S. up to the attending physician wherever you happen to be. A typical international life-flight can also cost upwards of $100,000 if you don't have any insurance. Air Ambulance Card is a membership fee-based program that is not based on "necessity" and they will send the nearest plane to get you out and back to a hospital. Surprisingly, the price is quite affordable considering the alternative. The annual cost is $225 for an individual and $325 for a family. I carry this one and hopefully, won't have to ever use it but the peace of mind it provides is worth the price.

Time and Date www.timeanddate.com

Want to know the time in Mozambique? Just log onto Time and Date and in a matter of seconds you can find the time you need. For those who do lots of international traveling, this site can help you answer the musical questions, "Does anybody really know what time it is?"

Auto Driveaway Company
www.autodriveaway.com

Auto Driveaway is a unique service that allows you to obtain free transportation by auto to a designated location. Essentially, a driver looking for transportation will call the company and find out if there are any owners who want to transport a car to where you are going. If so, and you are at least 23 years of age, then you place a cash deposit ($350) and you are on your way! The first tank of gas is free and food and lodging are at your own expense. Since 1952, Auto Driveaway has provided more than 30,000 North American travelers with transportation in more than 20,000 vehicles through their network of 40 offices. There is a refundable deposit of $300 and you need to have a good driving record but this is probably one of the least expensive ways to "see the USA in a Chevrolet," or any other makes for that matter.

Gas Buddy www.gasbuddy.com

With the price of gasoline fluctuating, how can you find out where to fill up for that cross country trip or just in your hometown? You log onto Gas Buddy of course. You can click on any state and then go to your local area to find the lowest cost of gas at any number of service stations.

European Rail System
http://www.eurail.com
http://swisstravelsystem.com
http://raileurope.com

The European Rail system is considered to be one of the most reliable on earth. For many it is the preferred method of transportation as you travel from point to point or country to country. Reaching speeds of over 100 MPH, some of these trains, like the French TGV (which stands for "tres grand vitesse") effortlessly take you to great destinations in record time. Since most rail stations are located near the town center, you can save money on cab fares and concentrate on your next place of interest. This websites have location information and pricing for single and multi-country Eurail passes.

In Switzerland you can obtain a Swiss rail pass via www.swisstravelsystem.com. For the one price of this you can have access to the trains, trams, lake transportation as well as access to about 400+ museums in the country. Another good site for rail transportation in Europe is www.raileurope.com.

CDC Travelers Health www.cdc.gov

When traveling outside the United States, this is one website you should visit. The Center for Disease Control lists things that you may want to know before you enter a country—like whether or not there is a viral outbreak of some sort, for example. Some of the recently listed cautions as of this writing were, of course, Ebola and other serious illnesses. This is also a good place to find out whether there are certain vaccinations required for the country you are visiting.

Dangerous Places www.comebackalive.com

In this day and age, there are obviously some places that you will want to avoid completely. This website will tell you in plain English which parts of the world are so dangerous that you may want to re-think your plans. There are also links here to specialty insurance such as ransom and kidnapping as well as the Black Flag Café, which is an interesting sounding name but Is really just a forum for high-risk travelers.

Outbreaks Global Incident Map
http://outbreaks.globalincidentmap.com/home.html

Let's face it. The world can be a dangerous place and knowing where to avoid might be as important as where to go. If you really want to become paranoid then you can logon to the Outbreaks Global Incident Map. This will show you, in real time, where nasty things are happening around the world. You can find everything from West Nile to biological incidents to Ebola. Maybe it's best not to look?

Travel Insurance
www.insuremytrip.com
http://www.ingleinternational.com
http://www.squaremouth.com

One of the problems with many travel insurance policies is that they tend to hide the details in the fine print. So you may think you can get you money back if you are sick, for example, but then the company tells you that the sickness has to be "life threatening." Insuremytrip.com provides you with comparisons for up to 18 companies so you can quickly see how they are different from one another. Prices vary and I have found better deals with lower cost policies that don't have such restrictive language. Always compare. Other similar products can be found at Squaremouth.com and specialty insurance at http://www.ingleinternational.com.

My Trip Journal www.mytripjournal.com

"First you do, then you tell. But imagine being able to do and tell at the same time!" These words briefly describe how this website works. The basic insurance is free but they also have a premium version with more features for only $99/yr. and a $29 version that will cover you for 60 days. You can create your own website, create maps, include photos and journal information so that your friends and family can share your experiences while they are happening. They have a very nice interactive display and their mapping system shows those who log on where you have been and where you are going, just like Rick Steve's.

Virtuoso® www.virtuoso.com

For some people, the thought of searching through endless websites can be daunting. For those who would rather deal with a good travel agent, then check out Virtuoso.com. These are pre-screened agents (probably in the top 1% nationwide), many of whom specialize in different destinations. Some do charge for their services but will work hard to earn your trust, and your business.

Airport Parking Reservations
www.airportparkingreservations.com

They show all of the details including ground transportation and services offered. One of the other benefits is that instead of just leaving your car at an airport lot, you can find a nearby hotel that, for a package price, will allow you to spend the night and then leave your car in their lot. Shuttle buses will then transport you to the airport and pick you up upon return.

Fly Cheap, Stay Cheap, Travel Cheap

Park, Sleep, Fly www.parksleepfly.com

This seems to be a partner website to airportparkingreservations.com where you can request quotes from most airport hotels for a room and parking. They will quote you a package price that includes the overnight room rate and up to 14 days of parking at the property. This saves on time and stress with trying to compete with the airport parking lots which may end up costing more than the hotel package price. They also offer a similar service if you are planning on taking a cruise.

Chapter Two
Airline Tips and Secrets

Airline Tips and Secrets

If you're like me, you probably think that airlines have become something of a necessary evil. Yes, you have to rely on them to get you from point A to point B, but when problems crop up, the experience can cause tempers to rise to the boiling point. Flight delays, cancellations, strikes, apathetic employees, and now time-consuming security measures, can test the resolve of the most patient flyer.

I recall a flight my wife and me were taking from Miami back to Colorado. When I suddenly realized that I didn't have my tickets, I went to the ticket agent, who was less than amused and wanted to charge me a hefty fee for the inconvenience and paperwork that this would cause him. Despite my pleadings, the agent still wouldn't budge. What to do? I followed one of his "rules of life": "When in doubt, climb the ladder."

Fly Cheap, Stay Cheap, Travel Cheap

In other words, a call to the airline's toll-free number and a request to speak to a supervisor resulted in newly issued tickets with no fee. The ticket agent was not so happy, but as I like to say (borrowing from Captain Kirk!), "I like to think that there are always possibilities." This is certainly true when it comes to airline travel.

In my years of traveling, I have come up with a number of tips on coping with the airlines. Here are some of them that we happily pass on to you.

• Begin your trip planning by calling the airline's toll-free number and asking for the lowest possible price. Some airlines give it to you right away, while others make you ask nicely! A price quote for roundtrip airfare from Denver to Los Angeles in January, for example, was $463.50. When we asked the agent to "fare shop" the lowest available price on that route, she told us that if we left on a Tuesday or Wednesday and returned on one of those days as well, the price would drop to $381.50, a savings of $82.00. Other airlines might have other days that make their computer spit out a lower fare. Advance purchases (usually 14 or 21 days before you'd like to travel) may also factor into the equation. Don't take the first answer as the gospel. Always ask for the lowest possible fare for your route, or to "fare shop" for the best price. Of course, you can then follow this up by going on airline search engines to see if you can do any better.

• If you can, be flexible. Vary your days and times of travel. Sometimes just modifying your date to include a Saturday night stay can lower your price.

• Compare. In the blink of a keystroke, Internet sites such as www.travelocity.com or www.expedia.com, can provide you with a good comparison of fares and schedules, right on-line.

• Check with smaller airlines that provide service to your destinations. Upstart companies like Jet Blue (www.jetblue.com) can save you up to 65% over larger competitors.

• Check nearby airports (at least when you're fare shopping). Instead of flying from Denver, check on prices from Colorado Springs. Skip the busy Los Angeles International Airport and check on Burbank, Santa Ana (John Wayne), or Ontario.

• Forget Washington, DC's Reagan National Airport or Dulles International and look at Baltimore-Washington International instead. You may find that you can save enough money for a rental car and hotel room if needed. And you may well be able to skip the crowds and commotion at

Fly Cheap, Stay Cheap, Travel Cheap

the larger airports. Most travel search engines provide alternative airport options.

• Enroll in frequent flyer programs. My wife and I have taken at least eight trips for free using our frequent flyer awards. A good website to explain how this works is www.frugaltravelguy.com. Remember, however, that blackout dates may apply when and where you want to go (it's unlikely, for example, that you're going to be able to use your frequent flyer miles for a Christmas jaunt that is 2 months away. And Hawaii may be much more difficult to get to than, say, Des Moines.) It pays to compare.

• The cheapest days to fly are usually Tuesday, Wednesday and Saturday with Wednesday being the cheapest overall. According to some travel experts, the best times to book are 4 am as well as right after lunch and dinner.

• When you are traveling, always carry copies of your passport, important documents, and medication prescriptions. If you lose your primary documents you will be glad that you had a backup in emergencies. Also, remember to keep these separate from your main papers. Another option would be to scan these documents and email them to your smartphone or pad so that you have a backup.

Fly Cheap, Stay Cheap, Travel Cheap

• European rail travel is great, but so is flying around the Continent. Check out www.europebyair.com for $99 one-way flights to more than 150 cities.

• Always pay for major travel expenses with a credit card. Depending on the card, this may offer some protection when problems arise. Many cards also include insurance and other perks by using their card.

• Whenever possible, carry on your luggage. Airlines can—and frequently do— lose bags, so bypass all of these headaches by packing sparingly and taking your luggage on the plane. If you are flying internationally, this will also save you time at customs. While others are hoping their bags appear on the carousel, you will be breezing your way to the checkpoints, on your way out of the terminal. The website www.onebag.com is a great resource for compact packing. Also check out space saving jackets and vests sold by Scottevest.com.

• Remember, if you do run into problems, always ask for a higher authority to have the best chance of getting the answer you want.

Fly Cheap, Stay Cheap, Travel Cheap

Now, back to the theme of the book...my Internet travel favorites. Here are some of my pet web picks for airline travel.

Online Booking Sites
Hotwire www.hotwire.com

If you're looking for the lowest prices, Hotwire may be just your ticket (so to speak!). They advertise that you can save up to 60% on hotel rooms. The catch is that they don't reveal the airline you'll be flying or the flight times until you actually book your ticket. Unlike some true auction sites, however, Hotwire will actually tell you the price before you decide to book. It also says that it will get you on the lowest- priced flight leaving between 6 a.m. and 10 p.m. on a particular day. A recent fare check from the Midwest to Los Angeles got me an airline quote of $376. On-line booking sites listed fares beginning at $389. Hotwire' s fare? An unbelievable $206, for a savings of at least $170. Best of all, the prices they quote include all taxes and airport fees.

Kayak www.kayak.com

Kayak allows you to search a variety of airline fees in a single step. Just input the locations and dates of travel, press a button, and the fare search begins. A handy flex calendar also shows you alternative travel dates that may be less expensive. Kayak.com is currently owned by Priceline.

Mobissimo www.mobissimo.com

Very similar to Kayak but seems to be more powerful and searches many other discounters including cheap tickets, one travel and others. It is web-based rather than software-based and offers a powerful way to compare one site vs. another. You can also compare many other sites from here like Expedia, Orbitz and others. I noticed that their latest website version does seem to have a lot of pop ups and sponsored ads but you should still be able to find good up-to-date comparison information for travel.

Booking Buddy www.bookingbuddy.com

If you have ever thought that it would be nice to have a single search engine that would allow you to simply search all of the other search engines, then you will like booking buddy. You simply put your to and from locations and dates, then click on the appropriate link (ie. Travelocity, Kayak, Hotwire, etc). Booking buddy will then take you directly to the appropriate website. You can search for air, hotels and rental cars all from this one location.

Fly Cheap, Stay Cheap, Travel Cheap

Adioso www.adioso.com

Sometimes using airline search engines can be a little confusing since they don't tend to function in the same way that people think. But what if there was a website that does? Enter Adioso. You can search for things in a more brain-friendly manner. So, if you are thinking about going to New York City next Friday, then you can simply search for NYC next Friday. Then Adioso will search for all the flights available for that time and date. If you want to travel someplace internationally for, say, $500 then you can simply search that way as well. So, no matter what is on your mind in terms of travel, Adioso seems to be smart enough to figure that out and put it together for you. It is a little hard to find this quick search button but it is in the upper left corner of their homepage. Sort of reminds me of an old move, "Open the pod bay doors, please HAL (2001, a Space Odyssey).

Sky Scanner www.skyscanner.com

Sky Scanner will search more than 1,000 airlines to find you the best deals. They can also do the same for rental cars and hotels. This website also has a function that will show you a chart of the highest and lowest dates of the month to book your flight.

Fly Cheap, Stay Cheap, Travel Cheap

Which Airline
www.whichairline.com

Which Airline searches all low cost airlines to and from a particular destination. This includes Ryanair, Easy Jet and others. If there aren't any niche airlines then it will show others. For example, searching from Denver to Vienna in December showed available flights on Lufthansa and a lower price on Swiss Air. What I particularly like is that they provide an easy to understand, color-coded bar chart showing the overall length of the trip and number of stops.

Route Happy
www.routehappy.com (App too)

The developers of Routehappy.com felt that there was more to an airline search than just the airline and pricing. They decided to rate searches according to happiness factors such as seats, amenities, flight duration, entertainment, power, Wi-Fi and fresh food. I checked a flight from Denver to Vienna and one of the flights was on Lufthansa with an overall 7.8 rating. The details showed me things like free back of the seat entertainment, and a 3-4-3 seat layout. Even though it told me this could be somewhat crowded it also included this helpful tidbit: "Little known fact: the aisles in the center section have half as many people climbing over you." Routehappy is a fairly new site but I like the *feel good* traveler information I am finding here.

Hipmunk www.hipmunk.com (App too)

Another new airline search tool that has appeared recently, Hipmunk searches thousands of fares and provides the information in a graphically pleasing way. It will show you, for example, the hard to see departure and arrival times using arrows as well as layovers and other useful data.

Fare Compare www.farecompare.com

Fare Compare is a fairly large website with lots of valuable travel information. It is run by Rick Seaney who is regularly featured as a travel expert on TV. You can search for airfares, deals, and get travel advice here. One of the things I like about Farecompare is the ability to search for deals from your home airport. Once you input the information you can search for deals according to a theme such as golf vacations, beach vacations, family fun destinations and more. This makes it quite easy to plan a getaway without having to navigate all over the place. They have a helpful where to go getaway map that shows you the prices to many cities around the world.

Fly Cheap, Stay Cheap, Travel Cheap

Bing www.bing.com

Bing has quite a links to pretty much everything but under the "more" tab you can find a travel link. If you click that you can then search for airfares. They have a price predictor that will show you within a week or so of your trip whether the prices are tending to rise or fall. Based on that, you can decide whether to purchase your tickets now or wait.

Tripit www.tripit.com

This is one of my favorite websites. Once you enroll for free you simply input all your travel plans, including your airline, hotel, rental car, attractions, meetings, etc. Tripit summarizes all your travel plans into one or two pages, including all those pesky confirmation codes. It will also color code plans according to category and put them into the right chronological order. What is even better is if you have an iPhone or iPad application, it will send your online plans to your phone making it unnecessary to have to carry all that paperwork when you travel. You can also send your abbreviated itinerary to your friends and relatives.

ITA Software http://matrix.itasoftware.com

ITA boasts a new technology that allows you to rapidly search every available fare combination. Computer engineers from M.I.T. developed this software in their "artificial intelligence laboratory." ITA gives you a good comprehensive look at current flights all across the board. You can log on as a guest to search the available fares. I searched for fares from Denver to Paris and it showed 14 different airlines that service that route along with advisories such as overnight flights and long layovers. This one is not very well known but easy and fun to use.

Expedia www.expedia.com

This is another good site that books air and other packages. Many companies like Expedia list special deals right on their homepage. You may see something that strikes your fancy even more than your original idea.

Orbitz www.orbitz.com

Orbitz claims to have the most airline "web-only" fares in the business. Like many other sites, you can book air only, or search for other travel packages, rental cars, and hotels.

Fly Cheap, Stay Cheap, Travel Cheap

Rates to Go www.ratestogo.com

This is another website owned by Orbitz advertising last minute hotel deals. I haven't used this one personally as it is fairly new but I did find a nice last minute 4-star hotel with good feedback in Times Square for $179 plus tax. Guess that is pretty good for New York City.

Smarter Travel www.smartertravel.com

Smarter Travel has a "step-by-step" airfare guide that allows you to search for Internet specials, current sales, on-line travel agents, travel auctions, consolidators, and more. You can even request periodic emails to keep you up- to-date regarding Internet specials. (Many of the travel sites, as well as the individual airlines, have e-mail newsletters with discounted promotional fares as well.) Smarter Travel Media LLC also owns airfarewatchdog.com
and bookingbuddy.com.

Pleasant Holidays www.pleasantholidays.com

This is a charter operation that has value deals on airfare, lodging and rental cars for destinations all over the world. They keep their prices low by negotiating the best deals with commercial airlines.

Fly Cheap, Stay Cheap, Travel Cheap

Priceline www.priceline.com

You can now use Priceline to obtain flight, hotel and vacation packages. Many people have found good deals on Priceline. In the case of hotels, you can name your own price and if accepted, they will reveal the name of the hotel.

Bidding for Travel
www.biddingfortravel.com
http://biddingfortravel.youku.com

One way to ensure that you do get the best deal on Priceline is to visit www.biddingfortravel.com. This site will give you insider information in the form of people who have already successfully bid on Priceline products. You can see how much they paid on hotels, and bid intelligently on Priceline. I recently found a person who bid on a hotel in downtown Denver on Priceline and posted their results on Biddingfortravel. Here is what they found:

Best Advanced Purchase Rate from hotel website was $107.10 + $15.79 = $122.89. I bid $55, which was rejected with offer to increase by $9 and adding another area. I increased $1 to $56, and won with total $70.94 price. My total savings after taxes/fees of $51.95, or about 42% best web rate.

Fly Cheap, Stay Cheap, Travel Cheap

Sky Auction www.skyauction.com

Like Priceline, Sky Auction lets you bid for flights. They've made it easy to use by categorizing the different areas in which you may bid. This includes Europe, the US and Canada, Latin America and Mexico, Asia, Australia, Africa, sun packages, and hot deals. I recently saw a business class airfare summer roundtrip auction from New York to Paris with a bid of $101.

Vayama.com www.vayama.com

Vayama has an incredible database of international flights to over 190 countries. Using an interactive map, travelers can view the prices from their home airport all over the globe. Just point and click to book the fare. I found a round trip flight from Denver to Paris for $679 in early March which was cheaper than the typical $900+ fares.

Yapta www.yapta.com

No, this isn't the sound your little dog makes in the middle of the night when it barks. The acronym stands for Your Amazing Personal Travel Assistant. The concept behind this website is for you to have a way to track when airline prices fall to an acceptable level. You can track flights before or after you leave and then see if you are eligible for a refund. They have a smartphone app as well that will let you know if you are eligible for a refund.

Europe by Air www.europebyair.com

Traveling within Europe doesn't have to be an expensive proposition. Europe by Air connects with a network of European travel partners where you can fly to many destinations for less than $100. Some recent hot fares I saw on their site included London to Nice for just $81 (including all taxes and fees) and Rome to Geneva for only $79.

Jet Blue www.jetblue.com

Jet Blue has a rapidly expanding network, which includes points on the east and west coasts. One-way tickets from Orlando to San Juan were only $79 plus taxes and fees at the time of this printing! One of the things we like best about Jet Blue is that each seat is leather and comes with its own TV! You can even take a virtual tour of Jet Blue's planes on the website. They have an easy to use interactive travel map and Jetblue Getaways with low-priced packages to many destinations. They have also introduced a new service called jetBlue Mint™ which is a sort of luxury coast to coast service with lay flat seats, better food and your own personal cubicle. Flights from LA to NYC were running $599 one-way at the time of this printing.

Flight Trackers
Flight View www.flightview.com

Flight View lets you access current flight status for almost any airline. In addition to viewing flight status, you can see radar imagery of conditions along the route. Flight View will not show data on flights that are on the ground. They have a handy dandy mobile app for iPhone or Androids as well.

Flight Stats www.flightstats.com

Another flight tracking website, this one also has a handy smartphone app. You can easily access maps showing delays from very low (solid green circle) to excessive (solid red circle). They have an airport zoom app that has loads of helpful information from airport amenities to interactive terminal maps.

Air Traffic Control System Command Center www.faa.gov

This site will give you a visual graphic display of major airports in the United States. A color-coding system will instantly tell you the status of any delays at a particular airport. This will range from delays of less than 15 minutes all the way to a closed airport. You can click on any listed airport to find out the local details. You will find the information under the air traffic tab and then scroll to flight information.

Frequent Flyer Programs
Boarding Area www.boardingarea.com

Basically this is a giant collection of blogs with all sorts of good information relative to frequent flyer programs, hotels awards, travel contests and more. Postings are typically done on a daily basis so you want to check back frequently so as not to miss important news.

Frugal Travel Guy www.frugaltravelguy.com

This is one of my favorite frequent flyer and award blogs. Rich Ingersoll and his wife have been around the world several times, all for free using frequent flyer and award miles. He updates his website daily and advises about the best tactics and offers to accumulate miles and points that you can use to start traveling for free. Make sure you read through the past archives to educate yourself before applying for credit card offers. Past discussions include how to check your credit score for free before you apply, protecting your credit and the right way to score miles using credit card offers without affecting your hard earned credit score. One year my wife and I applied for just a couple of the offers we saw here and in 3 month time, we amassed 500,000 miles between us. This was enough for two round trip fares to Hawaii with a bunch of points left over.

Mile Tracker™ www.miletracker.com

If you have ever tried to keep track of multiple frequent flyer accounts, you know how frustrating that can be. But, with Mile Tracker, you can easily organize all those miles into one nice screen. It also keeps track of all relevant changes in each of your accounts.

Seats www.seatguru.com

Okay, you've booked your flight and now you're ready to choose your seat. But, before you do, visit SeatGuru. They have seating charts for most domestic air carriers and will help you pick the best seat. Maybe you need extra legroom. Or you would like something away from noisy distractions. Whatever your preference, this site can save you from being frustrated while winging across the country with your knees wedged up against the seat in front of you. Want to know the best seat on the plane? The worst? This one will tell you all that and more.

Travelocity Last Minute Deals
www.travelocity.com

While the Travelocity website does have a great number of deals and search features, they also have a link for travel deals that lets you browse through almost a 1,000 different options such as airfares, hotels and vacation packages.

Chapter Three
Unique Lodging Ideas

Chapter Three
Unique Lodging Ideas

Once you figure out where to go, the next question is, "Where to stay?" Even if you want a five-star hotel, you don't necessarily want to pay five-star prices, do you? No, I didn't think so. Yes, you can call a hotel's toll-free number, but you are not likely to get the best deal by doing that. As with most of what I have been talking about in this book, your first stop should be the Internet. There you will find values galore, including many bargains offered by hotel chains.

If you are new to the world of computers and cyberspace, you might wonder how you would go about actually finding a particular website. Since most businesses try to list their company by their actual name, you can usually find them just by typing the name into the address line of your browser. If you wanted to find the Marriott Hotels, for example, chances are all you would have to do is type in the address line www.marriott.com (and chances are you're right!). This is a simple trick that works most of the time; when it doesn't, just go to your favorite "search engine":

www.yahoo.com
www.google.com
www.hotbot.com

are some of my favorites. Once there, all you have to do is type the name of what you're looking for and it will bring up anything with the words you indicated. So, if you're looking for discount hotels in Orlando, just type the words, "discount hotels Orlando," and you'll be shown a list of display hotels with the words "discount" as part of their advertising.

I've done some of the groundwork for you. Here are some of our favorite hotel reservation sites. It's not a complete list, but it will get you started.

Hotels.com www.hotels.com

Click on a city and you'll find a list of hotels offering significant savings. They claim to offer the best prices on more than 245,000 properties worldwide, including independent and chain properties.

Fly Cheap, Stay Cheap, Travel Cheap

Air BnB www.airbnb.com

This is a newer website but one that is becoming quite popular. People from all over the world can post accommodations on the website whether it is a spare room, loft, basement, apartment or anything else. Then you simply enter the city you want to search and you will find all sorts of reasonable accommodations. I found $15 rooms in NY and $18 rooms in Paris, France. They cover 34,000 cities in 190 countries with 600 of the accommodations located in castles! Compared to the cost of high-priced hotels, this one can provide HUGE savings to you.

Rocketmiles www.rocketmiles.com (App too)

What's better than just booking a hotel room while on vacation? Earning air miles, of course. With Rocketmiles you can do just that. Book your hotel on their website and choose which mileage program you would prefer. After you search the website will show you how many miles per night will be added to your frequent flyer account, up to 5,000 miles per night! They estimate that the "typical" frequent traveler would earn an extra 80,000 miles per year using Rocketmiles.

Couch Surfing www.couchsurfing.org

Do you have friends you haven't even met yet? According to the Couchsurfing website that is just the case. Once you register and create a profile you can create a conversation about the city you would like to visit. People who live in that city and who are also registered can view your profile and decide if they would like to host you. It's pretty much that simple. Accommodations don't necessarily confined to just a couch as many have rooms available as well. Try it out for yourself and be part of the global couchsurfing community.

Quik Book www.quikbook.com

Listed as one of Forbes "Best of the Web", Quikbook has several advantages over other hotel booking sites. First, they don't sneak in additional fees that can lead to "rate creep." You know, those annoying little extra fees that they tack on your bill to raise your rates. The other thing is that you don't have to prepay for most of their properties. This provides a little peace of mind knowing that somebody at the hotel can't charge your credit card if you don't show up on time or if you make a mistake in your day of booking. Their room rates are among the lowest in the industry.

Fly Cheap, Stay Cheap, Travel Cheap

Venere www.venere.com

Just point at an interactive map and you are well on your way to big savings on accommodations. Unlike many other websites, Venere offers not just hotels but a combination of 200,000 hotels, B & B's, and apartments worldwide. Once you decide on a destination, Venere will provide you with reader's reviews, a star rating, prices and a photo gallery. People who have used this website have told me that the booking process was easy and they got some fantastic deals on their trip.

Hotels Combined www.hotelscombined.com

Located in Sydney, Australia, Hotels Combined is a sort of a one-stop-shopping source searching multiple hotel search engines all across the Internet. . They search over 2 million hotel deals in over 120,000 destinations worldwide. The website is available in 39 languages and supports 120 currencies. Here you can just input your requested information once and Hotels Combined will check other sites such as Hotwire, Venere, Lastminute.com, Orbitz and a host of others. They must be doing something right since more than 300 million travelers visit this site each year.

Secret Scotland www.secret-scotland.com

Born out of some friend's frustration at finding the best things to see and do as well as the most interesting places to say in the country, "Secret Scotland" is the result. Tour guides are presented in the form of day-by-day itineraries with detailed directions to find the best of Scotland by means of the most scenic routes. They have some sample tours and quite a bit of off the beaten track highlights that shouldn't be missed.

Room Saver www.hotelcoupons.com

Search for thousands of hotels in the U.S. and Canada that offer discounts to travelers (up to 70% off). They have online coupons that you just print out or use the appropriate code when calling to book and have added a mobile app version.

Half-Price Directories www.entertainment.com

You've probably seen the local entertainment books that contain discount coupons offered by local merchants. The same company that produces those coupon books also offers a discount hotel book with savings of up to 50% off the "rack" room rate. A domestic coupon book typically costs $29.99, however, they do run specials. They have recently added a digital version of their books that also include things like dining, rental cars, airlines, and more.

Help Exchange www.helpx.net

This site is designed as sort of a cultural working exchange vacation. Their data base includes a free online listing of host organic farms, non-organic farms, farmstays, homestays, ranches, lodges, B&B, inns, backpackers, hostels and others who invite volunteer helpers to stay with them short-term in exchange for food and accommodation (board and lodging). As for how much time you have to invest, that will vary. Some owners will only ask you to work as little as 2 hours per day while others may require 6 hours or more. Browse through their listings and you are bound to see something you will like.

Home Exchange www.homeexchange.com

With over 55,000 listings in 150 countries this website offers home exchanges worldwide. If your home is vacant when you travel, then you may want to consider a home exchange. Essentially, you contact like-minded people who will trade their home for yours. Thousands of people do this successfully every year without a hitch. Most of the folks who trade homes will treat your property as if it were their own. They will also be mindful that you are in their house as well.

Fly Cheap, Stay Cheap, Travel Cheap

Homes are traded all over the world. Instead of staying in a cramped hotel room, you might be relaxing by your own pool on the Mexican Riviera.

Home Link International www.homelink.org

Home Link has homes available throughout the world and has a vast number of properties in their database. You are sure to find something that will fit your needs at this one-stop shopping website. The website also says that if you don't find an exchange through HomeLink in your first year as a HomeLink member, your second year's membership with us is free. A one-year membership is $89 but if you are a little unsure if this is for you, then for only $39 you can try it out for a year with the limit being you can only contacting those in the USA.

Caretaker Gazette www.caretaker.org

How would you like to stay in a great location for free? You can do just that as a caretaker. This on-line newsletter lists house-sitting opportunities from all over the world. They boast that they have over 130 caretaker listings in each issue with more than 700 worldwide; the cost of the newsletter is only $29.95 a year (online access). When I looked at the website, I saw caretaker opportunities in Hawaii, Australia, Belize, Jamaica, and even the Netherlands. They have also recently added an MSNBC video on their site about people who do this as an avocation.

Trusted Housesitters
www.trustedhousesitters.com

Here is another unique way to be able to travel around the world, experience different cultures, all while staying for free. The secret is called housesitting. Thousands of people each year list their homes on websites like trusted housesitters and look for reliable people to watch their property and often, take care of pets or animals.
Advertised as the perfect "staycation," you can find all manner of places to stay for free including farms, country homes, and city dwellings where you can experience the best of a destination while having most of your expenses covered.

The key to finding successful placement is to create a good profile listing. Homeowners can be somewhat leery of having strangers stay in their home so the best listings might include things like references, nice profile photos, police background checks and a good summary of who you are and why you might make a good house sitter.

There are many people doing this, some of whom are full timers. One such couple chucked their stressful city lifestyle, sold all their belongings and started housesitting all over the globe. They have an excellent website and Facebook page where they document their journeys and give advice for anyone considering this as a career. You can visit them at www.suitcasestories.com.

Hotel Confidential www.hotelconfidential.com

How would you like to make a few bucks the next time you visit a hotel? Impossible? Not at all. With Hotel Confidential, they want your smart phone video review and are willing to pay for it. The first step is to visit the website and request a particular hotel that you would like to review. If they approve it then you will take 4 short (less than 90 second) videos using your smart phone (examples on their site) and submit them. After that they will pay you $25 via Paypal. Pretty sweet huh?

Free Campgrounds www.freecampgrounds.com
If you are an RV owner, then you need to take a look at this site. With state by state listings, you can search for places to park your portable home for FREE! These may include locations such as Wal-Mart (in their parking lot, of course!), municipal parks, and state wildlife areas, to name a few. Some of the campsites do require minimal compensation but are still quite inexpensive.

Fly Cheap, Stay Cheap, Travel Cheap

Camping Card
www.campingcard.co.uk
www.vicarious-shop.co.uk

You can camp throughout the world for only 11, 13 or 15 Euro per night for w people at over 2700 campgrounds in 20 European countries. They advertise that you will pay less than the lowest price normally charged in low season. To order the card and their companion guide you would need to go to the vicarious shop website listed above.

Bed and Breakfast www.bedandbreakfast.com

Listing thousands of bed and breakfast properties all over the world, this is truly a one-stop shop for saving money on accommodations. What's even better that this site also lists homestays, country inns, guest houses, lodges, cabins, historic hotels, small resorts, guest ranches, farmhouse accommodations, and working farm and ranch vacations. You can search by country and/or city, theme or hot deals.

Evergreen Bed and Breakfast
www.evergreenclub.com

Billed as a "B & B for people over 50," Evergreen is a great way to save money on accommodations. Since 1982 Evergreen has provided hospitality in private homes at more than 2,000 locations in North America alone. The cost less than $25 day and the cost includes friendly conversation, sightseeing tips and, in most cases, breakfast. You do have to agree to host people in your own home but only when it is convenient for you. You may find yourself at a country home, lakeside cottage, golf course condo, or even a yacht! The current listings cover the U.S. and Canada.

Hostels
Hostelworld www.hostelworld.com

Although the word "hostel" is prevalent in their domain name, the site also features campsites, self-catering accommodation, B&B's and budget hotels and currently lists over 27,000 properties in more than 180 countries. This is one of the only sites where you can get a confirmed reservation at any number of hostels worldwide. Some of these are quite unusual including former prisons, tree houses, and jungle retreats.

Fly Cheap, Stay Cheap, Travel Cheap

Hostelling International
www.hihostels.com   www.hiusa.org

A hostel is a shared facility that allows guests to stay at a fraction of the cost of a typical hotel room. Located throughout the world, "hostelling" is a way to travel cheaply and meet like-minded people along the way. What type of accommodations can you expect? Hihostels has more than 4,000 hostels operating in 90 countries. Some are large, providing beds for a few hundred people, while others are quite small and can take only a few at a time. The price of membership is $28 for an adult and $18 for a senior. You can join online and their related website (www.hiusa.org) was much easier to navigate for this purpose. Here you can also activate your card and make reservations for your stay.

Hospitality Exchange www.hospex.net

Hospitality Exchange is similar to a home exchange but in this case, members offer each other the "gift of hospitality" in their homes. Listings give a brief biography of the owner and a summary of what they offer.   You can find something for every interest and learn a great deal from those who also love to travel.   One listing was for a bird sanctuary on Vancouver Island, B.C., another for a half acre in Sydney right next to a National Park.   They are primarily a

North American-based organization but you can find things abroad as well.

YMCA www.ymca.net

YMCAs have been around for a long time and offer cut-rate deals for travelers. Guests must be at least 18 years old unless otherwise noted in the listings. The ones listed on this website are for the United States and you can almost certainly find one near you. There is also an international database at www.ymca.int (see the sidebar: YMCA Hotels).

Global Freeloaders
www.globalfreeloaders.com

The definition on their website says it all—"GlobalFreeloaders.com is an online community, bringing people together to offer you free accommodations all over the world. Save money and make new friends whilst seeing the world from a local's perspective!" As the name implies, you are basically staying in like-minded people's homes for free and you can offer the same option. Check their site for all the "Ins and Outs" associated with this great offer.

Fly Cheap, Stay Cheap, Travel Cheap

TV Trip www.tvtrip.com

Have you ever wished you could see some actual video of your proposed hotel and neighborhood before you actually book it? Now you can. At Tvtrip.com, they had the ingenious idea of taking video cameras and filming in and around hotels around the world. Just click on a city and choose your property. Tvtrip.com will then take you on your own personal tour so you can really see what it might be like to stay there. To date they have 52,000 hotel video reviews on their site.

Room Key www.roomkey.com

Founded by six of the leading hotels, this website endeavors to match you up with your ideal hotel. They state that they will always offer you the lowest publicly available rate.

Campus Lodging www.university-rooms.com

There are so many colleges and universities throughout the world that it would be impossible to list them all. When schools are in session there are probably not many rooms available for short-term travelers. But, when the students have all gone back home, bargains can be had. University-rooms.com makes finding suitable campus lodging easy. You can find all the relevant information such as what type of

Fly Cheap, Stay Cheap, Travel Cheap

accommodations are available, amenities, nearby stores, ATM's and make reservations.

Another way is just to type the words, "campus accommodations" into a search engine and you will find a whole host of campuses that rent rooms during the off season. I found schools like Stanford, William and Mary and many others, all offering accommodations.

Monastery Stays www.monasterystays.com

This one is similar to university-rooms but exclusively offers monastery accommodations in Italy. You can find a reasonably priced convent or monastery with many offering bathrooms, breakfast and good locations within the city. You can book in right online, in English.

Chapter Four
Cruising for Pennies On the Dollar

Cruising for Pennies On the Dollar

Why do so many people fall in love with cruising? Well, just consider:

• On a cruise, you unpack only once. Compared to the "if this is Tuesday, it must be Belgium," kind of trip, cruising allows you—and your luggage—to stay put in your floating hotel.

• All your meals are included in the price of the cruise. Again, compared to the cost of eating three meals a day on a landlubber tour, cruising almost always comes out ahead. In fact, your biggest decision while on board may be which meal to skip. Most ships have so many dining options, including sumptuous midnight buffets, that you might find yourself gaining more than just new friends.

• If you get tired, hot, or hungry (although that's hardly going to be a problem!) in a port of call you can always go back to the ship, take a nap and head back into town (provided the ship is still in port, of course!) Don't laugh...too many people forget to check the ship's departure time and wind up waving from shore.

• Entertainment is also included in the price of cruising. Many cruise lines offer top quality Broadway-type performances along with other entertainment options such as karaoke clubs, dancing, late night comedy acts, and more. Many ships also have theme nights or special events—from cooking and wine, to jazz night, to nature explorations.

• Cruising gives you the opportunity to meet new people and develop lifelong friendships. Don't be surprised to see some of these same people on future cruises.

Now that I have hopefully whetted your appetite for cruising, I have just a few other words for you...hurricanes, seasickness, heat, humidity and occasional fires. No, I'm not trying to scare you or turn you off to the idea of cruising. I just want you to do what I didn't do before my first cruises—my homework!

It's important to do your research before you book your trip. With all of the many options available in cruising, you'll definitely be able to find the right cruise for you and your family. But there are a number of things you need to consider, besides your preferred ports of call. Do you want a cruise line that specializes in families? Non-smoking? How about one that has special theme cruises? A large ship? Or maybe a small ship?

There are numerous sites that will help you decide which ship is best for you, and save you money and let you cruise the seven seas like a king—all the while on a pauper's budget. Here are the sites I like the best.

Cruise.com www.cruise.com

Cruise.com is a large site that has a wealth of information about cruise rates at some of the lowest prices available. I saw a 7-night cruise to Alaska for just $299 p/p on Norwegian and many other good deals.

Freighter Travel www.cruisepeople.co.uk/
(Tel: +44 (0)20 7723 2450   UK: 0800 526 313)

Ever wished you could take an extended cruise to exotic ports of call without the usual crowds, dress codes, and formalities? Freighters carry not only cargo, but also small groups of passengers who enjoy sailing to such destinations as the Orient, the South Pacific, Australia, and New Zealand.

Fly Cheap, Stay Cheap, Travel Cheap

Instead of the usual 7-10 day excursions, these ships take their time, usually from 30-75 days.

About 90% of the vessels are container ships with others being multi-purpose or bulk carriers. You're not slumming it either when you go by freighter. Most have lounges with upholstered furniture, a library, self-service bars, a swimming pool, and more. Regular meals are the only planned activity and though they may not be gourmet in quality, they are varied, tasty, and well balanced.

This is a good cruising alternative if you want to spend longer times on a ship and if you don't like being constantly annoyed with things like art auctions, gambling lounges, overpriced drinks, etc.

You may find yourself developing lifelong friendships with the other passengers. Not hard to see why when you consider that the typical passenger load is from 2- 12 people.

The pricing varies but a good round number to plan on is about $100 per day per person.

Cruisepeople.co.uk are booking agents that can help you select the right freighter for your needs. You can email or call them (London time) but they are friendly and helpful. In addition to the regular freighter cruises they also offer Antarctic and expiation cruises, round the world jaunts as well as small and tall ship cruises. I would recommend them as a starting point over others I found online.

Cruise Compete www.cruisecompete.com

Why not let cruise companies compete for your business the same way that mortgage companies do? With Cruise Compete you request a quote and then a number of cruise companies will send you their best offer. Pick the one you like and you're on your way to smooth sailing.

Cruise 411 www.cruise 411.com 800 553 7090

Listed in Forbes Magazine's "Best of the Web," Cruise 411 boasts that it has the largest cruise database with discounts on the web. You can search by destination or by cruise line, and learn about last-minute deals, 2-for-1 offers, and more. Don't miss the individual ship information and the articles on cruising. At the time of this writing I found a 12 night Greek Isles cruise on Celebrity with balcony and onboard ship credit for just $1,499.

Best Fares www.bestfares.com

Best Fares has all kinds of great travel information on its site, including help in finding a cruise just right for you. The latest news in cruising is right here, from which ships are having their inaugural cruises, to 2-for-1 deals, special sailings, theme cruises, and more. By listing cruises and specials chronologically, you can stay informed of late-breaking cruise events. This information is listed on the "free" side of the site; paying members have access to even greater savings. Also, if you are a current or inactive member of the military, Best Fares was offering (at the time of this writing) up to 69% off Carnival Cruises rack rates to a host of destinations--Woo Hoo and thank you all for your service!

Cruisemates www.cruismates.com

Cruisemates is a wonderful site for researching cruise travel and bargain hunting. A library of information offers you articles on medical care at sea, interviews with cruise directors, the top ten bargain cruises, and much more. There are also helpful links for ship reviews, first-time cruisers, teens, chat, and side-by-side ship comparisons. You can also search their forums and find the most popular deals. I found this one recently that looked like a fantastic deal: Select 2014 Caribbean sailings on MSC Divina from only $249

Fly Cheap, Stay Cheap, Travel Cheap

(plus tax). Book Balcony (starting at $549), Suite, or MSC Yacht Club and receive $300 Shipboard Credit. Hurry, offer ends soon!

Teaching on a Cruise Ship
www.sixthstar.com Poshtalks.com

Have you ever wondered how all those people providing entertainment on board ships get hired? These websites are the ones you would go to if you are interested in teaching adult enrichment programs on board a ship. Sixthstar.com has openings for positions such as arts and crafts, special interest speakers, ballroom dancers, distinguished gents and more. Most of these have an administrative fee per day attached to them but this small cost is outweighed by the high cost of many of these cruises. If you have some talent, hop online and check out the requirements. Who knows, you could be cruising the seas for next to nothing while doing something that you love.

Other Cruise Websites

Many of the mega-sites offer great cruise packages that you should check out. You can often find great bargains by just looking at their "hot deals" listing. Some of these are priced so low that you wonder how they could afford to sail the ship! Since the cruise industry has an abundance of unsold cabins, they would much

Fly Cheap, Stay Cheap, Travel Cheap

rather fill them with customers who will spend money on other aspects of sailing—from drinking to gambling to photography, gift shops, and more. So take advantage of the fares that are being listed on these sites all the time.

www.travelocity.com
www.expedia.com
www.orbitz.com

Chapter Five

Entertainment Deals, Bargains, and Fun Galore

Entertainment Deals, Bargains, and Fun Galore

There are literally tens of thousands of websites that deal with the subject of entertainment. Trying to list most of these would be impractical, not to mention virtually impossible. And, of course, everyone's definition of "entertainment" is different. You may think that scuba diving is sheer entertainment, while your best friend thinks museum-hopping is just her cup of tea.

Since I can't include everything on my list, I've tried to offer a sampling that will get you started when planning your trip. Many of these offer discounts and most have links to other sites that have even more information. So let's have some fun!

Ticketmaster www.ticketmaster.com

Ticketmaster has been around a long time and offers many different choices for your entertainment palate. You can purchase tickets for music, sports, art, shows, and family events through their website. They also have a "Ticket

Deal" link that can save you big bucks, and is listed by city and state.

Undercover Tourist™
www.undercovertourist.com

If you are planning on visiting any of the Orlando theme parks then check out this website first. They have all sorts of valuable information to help you plan your visit including a green, yellow, red system of the best time of the day to visit the parks. You can also find discount tickets, smart phone apps and information about how to skip the long lines that tend to form during the peak season. The site covers Epcot®, The Magic Kingdom®, Hollywood Studios™ and the Animal Kingdom.

Playbill www.playbill.com

Planning to go to New York? Check out Playbill on-line for Broadway, off Broadway, regional, and other entertainment shows. They have a member's only section that allows you to obtain discount tickets and special offers for top-rated productions. They also have features where you can read about the latest happenings in the world of entertainment.

Theater Development Fund www.tdf.org

Operating since 1973, the Theater Development Fund (TDF) is the largest non- profit service organization of its kind for the performing arts in the United States. They sell discounted tickets for Broadway, off Broadway, dance, and music events. They advertise tickets that are 50 to 70 percent lower than standard ticket prices (plus a small service charge). The only catch is that these tickets are only available at one of their booths, located either in Times Square, the South Street Seaport or downtown Brooklyn. In addition to the day of performance tickets, a limited number of matinee tickets are sold one day prior to a performance, again at their locations at Times Square, 47th Street and Broadway, and at the South Street Seaport.

Wikitude www.wikitude.com

This app lets you augment your reality by showing you on your smartphone or iPad what is around you. Simply point your camera device and Wikitude will show you nearby hotels, restaurants, attractions and more. It can connect to Yelp, provide directions and even tell you monetary exchange rates just by taking a picture of your money.

Fly Cheap, Stay Cheap, Travel Cheap

Pocket Earth www.pocketearth.com

This helpful little app literally opens up the world to you in the form of interactive worldwide maps. The problem with most of these, in terms of travel, is that they use up a lot of data roaming fees if you want to use them overseas. Not pocket earth. You download the maps ahead of time and then, when you need to use them, they are available offline without any fees! The maps also include thousands of points of interest like hotels, restaurants, tourist sites, bus stops and more.
iTranslate www.itranslate.com

Don't speak the language in a certain country? No problem, iTranslate has you covered. Just type or speak the word or phrase into your phone and the app will provide it on your screen and say the correct pronunciation for you at the same time.
City Search www.citysearch.com

Most cities love to show you their best, virtually speaking of course. With City Search you can link to most of the larger metropolitan areas of the US. Once you find your city of interest, the sky's the limit. You can typically find everything that a city has to offer including food, lodging, movies, and attractions. You can read reviews of others and/or post your own.

Museums

www.museumsusa.org/
http://www.huffingtonpost.com/tag/weird-museums/
www.museumspot.com

There are museums all over the world. Some are straightforward (art, science, etc.) while others are offbeat and quirky such as railroad museums, voodoo museums, and more. Here's a short list and description of some of the more unusual museums out there:

Museum of Dirt—Yes, dirt. Take a virtual tour of historical dirt, vanity dirt, and even the history of dirt. Sure to contain some "dirty" pictures.

The Sherlock Holmes Museum—Bet you didn't think there was anything really located at 221-B Baker Street. Not true. Here you can find a museum dedicated to the famous detective and his creator, Sir Arthur Conan Doyle.

Burlingame Museum of Pez—This is listed as both a "real world" museum and a virtual one as well. Dedicated to all of us who grew up with those little plastic devices that allowed us to eat candy out of the heads of cartoon characters.

Fly Cheap, Stay Cheap, Travel Cheap

The International UFO Museum—Located, of course, in Roswell, NM you can come and decide for yourself if what happened there years ago was fact or fiction.

Zoos Around the World
http://www.bellaonline.com/subjects/6930.asp

Want to take the kids and family to see exotic animals? Then log on to this website and start exploring the world of fish, reptiles, birds, and other creatures. The Dallas World Aquarium and Zoological Gardens, for example, boasts a rainforest filled with birds, monkeys, and even jaguars. You can also learn about dolphins and killer whales in the marine park.

Theme Park Maps
http://www.themeparkbrochures.net/

If you have ever wondered what a theme park looks like before you get there, then check out this site. Over the years they have collected color maps of many of the country's top attractions including Knott's Berry Farm, Six Flags Magic Mountain, Busch Gardens, MGM Studios, Walt Disney World, and many more.

Fly Cheap, Stay Cheap, Travel Cheap

Airsickbags www.sicksack.com

Some people collect stamps and others, well...they collect airline sickness bags. You can view, donate or swap online unless you feel this isn't your bag.

Roller Coaster Data Base www.rcdb.com

If your idea of "entertainment" is blasting off at 60 mph into a series of turns and rolls, then you need this site. The Roller Coaster Data Base has information and statistics on more than 6,800 roller coasters throughout the world. There are many pictures and helpful comments about the different parks and coasters that will leave you dizzy before you ever get to the park.

Ghost Towns www.ghosttowns.com

Yes, the Wild West is gone but relics of the past still remain at many locations in the U.S. With several clicks you can zero in on your state and then your local community to see where Ghost Towns are located. You might be surprised to find some of these lurking in areas that you never imagined and find yourself taking a drive to explore these abandoned historic towns.

Fly Cheap, Stay Cheap, Travel Cheap

City Pass www.citypass.com

With this one book of coupons, you can have access to the best offers cities like New York, Boston, Philadelphia, Toronto, and Chicago. You purchase a passbook that contains the top attractions and then head straight to the front of the line while saving money at the same time. The New York City Pass includes discount admission to American Museum of Natural History, Guggenheim Museum, The Museum of Modern Art, Empire State Building Observatory, and The Statue of Liberty & Ellis Island or the Circle Line Sightseeing Cruises, So far, more than 13 million people have purchased city passes.

Knott's Berry Farm www.knotts.com

Knott's Berry Farm gets its own listing for one reason—I like it there! They have a great variety of rides set an "Old West" family atmosphere. Located in Anaheim, California, Knott's Berry offers discounts that can usually be found at local chain supermarkets and on their website.

As long as we're already at Knott's Berry Farm, here's my favorite part, and one of the things I miss most about Southern California—Mrs. Knott's Chicken Restaurant. Since 1934, Mrs. Knott's has been making some of the best fried chicken you'll ever taste. More than 20,000,000 dinners have been served to guests at the park. With your four pieces of country-fried chicken, you'll also get chilled cherry rhubarb, salad with their famous French dressing, buttermilk biscuits with boysenberry jam, and mashed potatoes with country gravy. Hungry yet?

Las Vegas www.lasvegas.com

Since there are so many discounts and "comps" (freebies!) available in Las Vegas, I've chosen to list this "entertainment" destination by itself. This website can provide just about anything you need for fun and adventure. Their entertainment link will list every show currently playing as well as a description and price. You can search for hotels and find prices for every budget, some as low as $39 per night in some months. If you gamble, then consider obtaining the casinos' "player cards." Depending upon how much dough you blow, you can start earning comp drinks, meals, and more.

Fly Cheap, Stay Cheap, Travel Cheap

Las Vegas Advisor www.lasvegasadvisor.com

I saw the person who started this website on TV years ago and it was quite fascinating. Using his knowledge and savvy of this town Anthony Curtis used coupons and special deals to actually stay there for free and even come out a few dollars ahead. Now he offers the same sort of expertise to you in the form of his newsletter and coupons. Let the savings begin!

Tourist Florida www.touristflorida.com

Literally everything about Florida from A-Z is listed on this website. You can tour the Kennedy Space Center, learn about Boggy Creek airboat rides, and see the Florida Zoological Park.

**Orlando Attractions
www.orlandoattractions.com**

Since Orlando is the hub of tourist activity, here is a site that will allow you to explore the best that this city has to offer. Everything from great water parks to Disney World to dining, golf, and beaches.

Unclaimed Baggage
www.unclaimedbaggage.com

Since this chapter is about saving money and entertainment, we didn't want to overlook what is for many their PRIMARY form of entertainment—shopping! Is there a way to get rock bottom prices on all kinds of merchandise? You bet. Unclaimed Baggage, in Scottsboro, Alabama, is where lost luggage goes when it can't find a home. Visit this site for big savings on jewelry, electronics, sporting goods, cameras, and of course, baggage. They used to sell their items online but alas, now you have to go to Scottsboro ad visit their 40,000 square foot facility to shop.

Roadtrippers www.roadtripppers.com

Roadtrippers allows you to create custom itineraries based on a particular theme. If you want to locate the best burgers in Southern California, for instance, just input that and this site will bring up a map of all the juicy burgers located in this area. You can do the same for museums in Cleveland, Greek food in Ohio and just about anything else. You can also create a road map trip from point A to B and Roadtrippers will show you all of the attractions and restaurants along that route. Their new technology allows you to sync to your iPhone or iPad for turn-by-turn navigation.

Fly Cheap, Stay Cheap, Travel Cheap

Xcom Global www.xcomglobal.com

If you travel internationally you know that cell phone roaming fees can be exorbitant. Xcom Global has portable wireless devices for rent that will keep you connected and save you money. They offer no roaming fees and each device will be pre-programmed for the country or countries you are visiting. Once they are activated they will connect to your laptop or phone allowing you Wi-Fi access no matter where you are. Daily rates start at $14.95 but check their website for full pricing details.

Movie Query www.mrqe.com

If you're a movie buff, check this out. On Movie Query, you can find multiple reviews for almost any movie, past and present. More than 100,000 titles are listed. So if you aren't sure you want your kids seeing the latest "R" rated movie, just log on and read what the critics have to say before you say, "No way!"

Chapter Six
Special Interests

Special Interests

Just as no two trips are alike, no two travelers are alike. Some crave sand and sun, others want to spend time on the links; still others wouldn't think of traveling without their pooch. Whatever special interests or needs you have, there is bound to be a website just for you. Here are some we think are especially helpful.

For the Physically Challenged
Accessible Journeys www.disabilitytravel.com

Since 1985, Accessible Journeys has designed tours especially for travelers with disabilities. Whether you are looking for a cruise that is wheelchair-friendly or are looking for a companion with similar disabilities, Accessible Journeys has what you need.

Emerging Horizons
www.emerginghorizons.com

As our society ages, the need for sites like this will become more pronounced. The main focus here is to provide assistance to wheelchair users and slow walkers. The author, Candy Harrington, also has several entire books on this subject so now, mobility disabilities don't have to be a barrier to a love for travel.

Access-Able Travel Services
www.access-able.com

Another website that caters to the disabled. You'll find information on mature travel, disability magazines, access guides, and wheelchair travel. You can find links to world destinations, cruise ships, and travel agents who specialize in accessible tours.

Society for Accessible Travel & Hospitality
www.sath.org

This site covers issues related to the disabled.

Beach Lovers
Dr. Beach www.drbeach.org

Each year this self-proclaimed beach survey expert lists his picks for the best beaches in the United States. Using 50 different criteria, Dr. Beach rates beaches for their cleanliness, quality of sand, and even the height of the waves. If you are searching for that perfect sandy piece of paradise, give Dr. Beach a try.

Surfline www.surfline.com

Surf's up dude! If you're planning to head to the beach and want to know how the waves are breaking and the condition of the surf, then check out Surfline. They have free reports, surf cams and forecasts for Hawaii, California, Florida, the Caribbean, and the East Coast.

Go Rving!
RV America www.rvamerica.com

Thousands of Americans own RVs. What could be easier than moving your home to a new location when the mood strikes? RV America has many different resources dedicated to this mobile lifestyle.

Volunteer Vacations

A number of organizations and travel companies sponsor volunteer vacations that can range from a few days to a few months. Teach English abroad, rehab a hiking trail in a national park, participate in an archaeological dig, work on an organic farm...the options are many, and are growing every day. Check out some of these sites.

Fly Cheap, Stay Cheap, Travel Cheap

**Volunteers-In-Parks, National Park Service
www.nps.gov/volunteer**

Global Volunteers www.globalvolunteers.com

**Volunteer Vacations, American Hiking Society
www.americanhiking.org**

Sierra Club Outings www.sierraclub.com

**Habitat for Humanity Global Village Program
www.habitat.org/gv**

**World-Wide Opportunities for Organic Farms
www.wwoof.org**

**Specialty Travel
InfoHub www.infohub.com**

This website offers a large variety of specialty travel options, 20,000 of them in fact. You can take guided or individual tours ranging from Active and Adventure to Romance to Sports or Culture and History. They have a nice breakdown of categories that will make your next vacation planning experience more meaningful.

Fly Cheap, Stay Cheap, Travel Cheap

Shaw Guides www.shawguides.com

Why take just an ordinary vacation when you can take one with meaning and purpose? Shaw Guides offer more than 6,000 sponsored links to learning vacations, creative and career programs worldwide. You can learn about cooking, food and wine, photography, language, golf, art and much more at any number of interesting locations throughout the world.

Airline Meals www.airlinemeals.net

If you are lucky enough to actually be served a meal these days, then you can stroll through their online photo gallery and see what's on the menu for any airline A-Z.

Pet Lovers
Pets Welcome www.petswelcome.com

Have you ever wanted to travel with your pet but didn't want to leave it at a kennel? With Pets Welcome, you don't have to. They have access to more than 25,000 hotels, B & Bs, ski resorts, campgrounds and beaches that are pet- friendly. "Come on Mr. Bigglesworth, we're going on vacation."

Fly Cheap, Stay Cheap, Travel Cheap

Senior Travel

Senior travelers may be entitled to special discounts through certain organizations, and may also prefer trips that are geared to their particular interests or activity level. Here are a few of the most useful sites geared to senior travelers.

USAA Insurance www.usaa.com

They have travel discounts and some requirements for membership such as active or retired military.

Evergreen Club
www.evergreenclub.com.

For just $25 for two, you can stay in a host home which includes breakfast at 2,000 locations in the U.S. and Canada. Annual membership is $75.

Seniors Home Exchange
www.seniorshomeexchange.com

Elderhostel-Now apparently called
Road Scholar www.roadscholar.org

Eldertreks www.eldertreks.com

Senior Summer School
www.seniorsummerschool.com

Walking the World
www.walkingtheworld.com

The Great Outdoors

If you harbor fantasies of participating in the Eco-Challenge, or just prefer spending your vacation outdoors, these sites will help you plan your own adventure trip.

www.Away.com
www.MTSobek.com
www.Iexplore.com
www.GORP.com
www.outdoors.org
www.outdoor-resources.com
www.BikeHike.com
www.us-parks.com
www.nationalparkhotelguide.com

Snow Bunnies

If schussing down the slopes spells heaven for you, you'll want to check out these sites.

www.ifyouski.com
www.ski.com
www.onthesnow.com

Fly Cheap, Stay Cheap, Travel Cheap

Golfing

Many travelers don't think a vacation is complete unless a set of golf clubs is involved. To find the perfect course for you, visit these sites.

www.worldgolf.com
www.resort-golf.com

Student Travel
Student Universe www.studentuniverse.com

This site is dedicated to offering reduced rates on air travel for students as well as faculty members. Started by a student in 1992, Student Universe is one of the only online travel websites dedicated to offering lower rates exclusively for the academically inclined.

Singles Travel Service
http://www.singlestravelservice.com/

There are many singles out there who would like to find a way to travel with like- minded people rather than being amongst a group of married and otherwise committed couples. The average age is between 30-60 but they have had people in their 70's. They will match up rooms with travelers on a first come basis and take personal preferences into consideration. Their motto is: "Give us a week and we'll give you a vacation you won't forget."

Fly Cheap, Stay Cheap, Travel Cheap

You're on your way!

Congratulations, you are now ready to fly cheap, stay cheap and travel cheap! We hope you have enjoyed this journey through the money saving world of the Internet. And with diligent use, your future travel and vacations can now be affordable, unique and surprising. But most of all affordable. Bon voyage, and don't forget to write!

Ron Stern presents this material in his popular talks, *Fly Cheap, Stay Cheap, Travel Cheap, Frequent Flyer Goldmine, Beginning Digital Travel Photography* and *How to be a Travel Writer: The Easy Way.* You can read more about these on his website at www.ronsterntravel.com.

To schedule Ron as a speaker at your next meeting or event, call (970) 227-9270.

Please visit Ron Stern's website at:
www.globalgumshoe.com

And his Facebook page at:
www.facebook.com/globalgumshoe